Mastering
Martial Arts

A Complete Guide to

KUNG FU

ANTONELLO CASARELLA
ROBERTO GHETTI

Enslow Publishing
101 W. 23rd Street
Suite 240
New York, NY 10011
USA
enslow.com

Published in 2018 by Enslow Publishing, LLC.
101 W. 23rd Street, Suite 240, New York, NY 10011

Library of Congress Cataloging-in-Publication Data

Names: Casarella, Antonello, author. | Ghetti, Roberto, author.
Title: A complete guide to kung fu / Antonello Casarella, Roberto Ghetti.
Description: New York, NY : Enslow Publishing, 2018. | Series: Mastering
  Martial Arts | Includes bibliographical references and index. | Audience:
  Grade 7-12.
Identifiers: LCCN 2017005210 | ISBN 9780766085411 (library bound)
Subjects: LCSH: Kung Fu—Juvenile literature. | Martial arts—juvenile
  literature.
Classification: LCC GV1114.7 C378 2018 | DDC 796.815/9—dc23
LC record available at https://lccn.loc.gov/2017005210

Printed in the United States of America

To Our Readers: We have done our best to make sure all websites in this book were active and
appropriate when we went to press. However, the author and the publisher have no control over
and assume no liability for the material available on those websites or on any websites they may
link to. Any comments or suggestions can be sent by e-mail to customerservice@enslow.com.

Photo Credits: Cover © leungchopan | Shutterstock

All interior images © by DVE Publishing, worldwide, branch of Confidential Concepts, USA.

Contents

Prologue

Kung fu and martial arts have been part of Chinese culture for centuries, but in the past few decades they have taken on unexpected relevance in our society.

The growth of the Chinese community abroad has brought the practice of kung fu to every corner of the world. Whereas kung fu used to be jealously guarded and was only taught within the community, in the past forty years, its teaching has opened up to Westerners.

The popularization of kung fu is not merely linked to the migratory flows of the Chinese community: in Europe, there are many schools founded by local masters, trained both in China and in their country of origin.

Thanks to some great productions, cinema has also helped popularize, among Western countries, the ideal of the warrior man who fights against evil using the simplest weapons—his hands and feet—with such skill that it is near perfection and goes beyond violent moves.

In reality, the practice of kung fu does not correspond to that mysterious image that the cinema has promoted, but it is based on precise fighting techniques that can be learned with perseverance and dedication in gyms and kung fu schools led by professionals who have a deeper knowledge of this discipline and know our personal characteristics.

Even if we have a trainer at our disposal in our sports center, we cannot always consult him or her about all our doubts. Therefore, this book will be a great help to those people who want to get the most out of their training time.

Its author, Master Antonello Casarella, is a kung fu expert and enjoys great prestige among European kung fu masters.

This book provides readers with all of the resources that they need in order to master this discipline, as well as advice and tips that will ensure a safe and efficient course of study.

Casarella introduces readers to the history, philosophical foundations, and varied styles of kung fu and presents the foundational moves in a comprehensive format. The instructions are clear; the description of the moves, techniques, and combinations are thorough; and the image selection is exhaustive and unequaled.

Kung fu enthusiasts will find here a manual that they should not do without. Writing and publishing this guide is a great initiative that all kung fu lovers will highly appreciate.

XAVIER MOYA GARCÍA
Wushu Kung Fu World
Champion (Beijing, 1991)
Full Contact World
Champion (1997-2000)

Introduction

Kung fu, or *wushu*, is a typical manifestation of Chinese culture, one of the most ancient and most complex civilizations of the world. As part of this culture, kung fu is equally ancient and complex, and its fragmentation into many different styles and methods makes it hard to classify and describe the techniques, which sometimes are markedly different depending on each school. We are aware that exploring the vast technical repertoire of kung fu is a difficult task, and therefore it is not easy to give due importance to the breadth of the discipline in the limited space of a book.

Kung fu is often surrounded by a halo of mystery that arises from the unclear and unscientific way in which it is presented. We will approach this topic from a technical perspective and attempt to dispel some of

the surrounding folklore that fires the imagination but distracts from the technical reality of the discipline.

While it can be tempting to link kung fu to the improbable feats one views in movies, kung fu has no secrets or magical techniques. It is a discipline that has a wide and deep vision of martial arts, one that minds the personal limits of its practitioners and teachers.

In this book, we will discuss the topic in a way that we hope is illuminating for both seasoned practitioners and novices alike. Common moves and the fundamental techniques will be presented in combinations that are accessible to readers of all experience levels.

Our wish is that all kung fu enthusiasts will find encouragement in this book to dig deeply and improve their technique, capturing the true essence of this superb martial art.

Transcription and Pronunciation of Chinese Words

China's national language is Mandarin, or Putonghua, but there are many dialects, and some of them are very different from the official language, such as Cantonese or Fujian's dialects.

That's why it happens that, especially in kung fu styles practiced in Hong Kong and southern areas, terms that come from southern dialects are used to describe positions and techniques. Especially in the past, this created problems and confusion. Fortunately, things are changing in China and in the rest of the world, and most practitioners of kung fu now use the national language. It often happens that a technique has different names depending on the style, which creates confusion for those who are not familiar with the Chinese language.

In order to avoid such confusion, in this book we use the most common name for the presented technique, along with its translation. Regarding names, we have used the official Chinese transliteration system called the Pinyin alphabet (with a few exceptions for the term "kung fu," which is "gonfu" according to the Pinyin alphabet).

Origins and History

Martial arts are one of the typical expressions of Chinese spirit and culture.

Wushu, known in the West as kung fu, evolved in parallel with the history of this fascinating country, an immense territory always marked by wars against invaders and bloody internal fights.

The feudal sociopolitical organization, which China didn't leave until the beginning of the twentieth century, has always motivated the community to autonomously anticipate the need for its own defense. Hence, many fighting systems evolved, each one with its own characteristics according to the technical requirements; the geographic, cultural, and ethnic frame; and lastly, the physical and psychological characteristics of each student.

In China, during the Warring States period (453–222 BCE), the passion for weapons and martial arts was transmitted among the military and the people, and many written testimonies about men's and women's skills and achievements have remained. There were even competitions organized to regulate the political relationships between the different states.

During the Han dynasty (206 BCE–220 CE), martial arts developed and acquired a more sporty character; for example, the first rudimentary protective gear appeared in competition. Weapons improved, in particular the double-edged sword, which experienced great development.

During the Tang era (618–907 CE), martial arts flourished. Thanks to a new examination system to

The renowned master Kuo Yun Shen in a rare period photograph (nineteenth century) during combat, in the times of the Qing dynasty.

select military officers, many kung fu masters were able to obtain prestigious positions and higher income. The practice and study of martial arts was encouraged in all levels of society.

In the times of the Song dynasty (960–1279 CE) and the later Ming dynasty (1368–1644 CE), kung fu had a great diffusion among the people. Also, by this time many schools and associations were created, often confronted in order to prove their prestige.

In this period *leitai* became very popular, a competition with bare hands in an elevated fighting area in which the fighter was considered defeated when he suffered a knockout or if he was thrown outside the fighting ground by the adversary. It was not uncommon that the challenges turned into a duel to the death.

The Manchu dynasty of the Qing (1644–1911 CE) saw the rise of new styles that are still practiced today, from *taiji* to *bagua* and from *tongbei* to *tanglang*. This period also saw a rise in secret societies such as the White Lotus and the Righteous and Harmonious Fists, which were created to defeat the unpopular ruling class and restore the Ming dynasty.

Kung Fu and Wushu

"Kung fu" is the most well-known term among Westerners when referring to Chinese martial arts. However, "wushu," which literally means "martial arts," is more commonly used in China. In this book, we will use both terms interchangeably. In China, "kung fu" doesn't apply solely to martial arts; the term is also used to describe anything that requires effort and perseverance to be achieved. "Kung fu" can be translated as "the result of hard work" or "improving through study." Thus, various pursuits such as a bachelor's degree, a work of art, or a difficult business venture—activities that require a person's maximum effort—can all be considered kung fu.

Many fighters were thrown in jail or executed for subversive acts.

Shaolin monasteries in the regions of Henan and Fujian in the south were destroyed. In 1727, the popular practice of kung fu was forbidden.

Many kung fu students and some famous masters died in the Boxer Uprising, the xenophobic movement connected to the Righteous and Harmonious Fists.

With the revolution of 1911, the modernization of Chinese martial arts began, also due to the cultural exchange with Western countries, which at that time were disputing the political and economic power in some areas.

In 1919, the association of the famous master Huo Yuanjia— Jing Wu—was founded in Shanghai. The association aimed to overcome the barriers among the different styles and encourage a new, modern, and scientific way to study martial arts. Since the founding of the People's Republic of China, wushu has experienced later transformations.

In the 1950's, the State Sports Commission started a new redefinition program that was designed to regulate martial arts. It discouraged the practice of traditional wushu in favor of popularizing wushu as a state-moderated sport. However, despite this pressure, traditional wushu survived, as people continued to secretly practice it during the period of the Cultural Revolution.

During the 1970's and 1980's, the government carried out a great effort to turn wushu

The practice of kung fu is recommended as early as childhood: it will improve balance, coordination, and strength.

into an international sport by standardizing some styles and exalting the gymnastic and acrobatic moves to the detriment of the purely martial ones.

Currently, the Chinese government is encouraging the creation of schools, associations, and groups of study and research regarding traditional wushu, promoting its recovery and appreciation.

Traditional and Modern Wushu

Today, martial arts can be divided into two big categories: traditional wushu and modern wushu.

Traditional wushu usually refers to schools and styles practiced outside the institutional sphere in China, but also in Taiwan and the rest of the world.

Kung Fu's Popularity in the West

When the first kung fu movies made in Hong Kong appeared in our cinemas in the 1960s, sociologists and intellectuals took the trouble of analyzing and explaining the success of these undeniably bad movies. The secret was that they spoke about men and women who reacted to the abuses to prisoners using their skilled practice, their tough discipline, and special techniques with which they achieved heroic, nearly supernatural deeds. They were romantic heroes who embodied strong individual values often forgot in modern societies; values often debatable—such as a sense of vengeance—but nevertheless important to the reaffirmation of the individual and his most noble virtues, through the means that we all possess, our body and our will.

In this category, we can find at least thirteen different schools and styles. In China, traditional wushu is also called "popular wushu," since it is considered a product and heritage of popular culture.

By contrast, modern wushu is the result of an attempt to standardize the traditional styles with the support of the government of the People's Republic of China. This process, which began in the 1950's, has taken wushu to the category

A phase of a choreographed combat that shows a fighter confronting three adversaries.

of a high-level sporting discipline. Competitive wushu includes several different disciplines:

1. *Taolu*, "form": Taolu is the execution of a series of continuous techniques that simulate an imaginary combat against one or more adversaries. Today, in taolu competitions different groups can be identified:

- *Chang quan*, the synthesis of the most important northern schools
- *Nan quan*, the synthesis of the most important southern schools
- *Taiji quan*, the most-practiced modern style
- *Xingyi* and *bagua*, two internal styles
- *Tongbi* and *pigua*, two external styles

- Imitative styles, styles that imitate animals, such as "eagle claw boxing," "monkey boxing," or "praying mantis boxing"

2. *Duilian*, "choreographed fight": Combat simulation between two or more adversaries, armed or unarmed.

3. *Sanda*, "free fighting sport": Two protected adversaries fight using fist, kick, and fighting techniques.

4. *Tuishou*, "pushing hands": It is a typical exercise of taiji quan (tai chi) used with the aim to unbalance the opponent and throw them outside the fighting ground. In order to achieve this, you must not use brute strength or grab your opponent, but use your own skill and the force of your adversary.

Kung Fu in Cinema

By Stefano Di Marino

Since the dawn of the twentieth century, popular Chinese cinema has exploited martial plots and techniques.

In the 1950s, a series of movies inspired by a real character, Wong Fei Hung, became very popular in Hong Kong. He was a famous master of Canton who lived at the end of the nineteenth century and the beginning of the twentieth century.

The real martial arts cinema boom was in the 1960s and the 1970s. At first, it was the *wuxiapian* movies, stories of wandering knights and swordsmen originating from the

Mandarin literary tradition (of Shanghai) and brought to Hong Kong thanks to the talent of directors such as King Hu and Zhang Cheh.

In these movies, we witness fantastic situations in which the protagonists are often flying and are able to create flows of magical energy. These are full-length period movies that have barely reached us and are little appreciated by the Western public.

On the other hand, the West was very enthusiastic about a second martial trend, *gongfupian*, which consists of more modern and real stories in which you could finally see kung fu practiced with bare hands. This new trend had an immediate success in Hong Kong, but we probably would have never heard of it if it weren't for *King Boxer*, which reached a cinema in Beirut by accident and shattered the expectations of the box office.

This is how kung fu movies entered the Western world and paved the way for Bruce Lee, who shot *The Big Boss, Fist of Fury, Way of the Dragon*, and *Game of Death* and for a short period became an idol for all enthusiasts.

After his death, the circumstances of which many consider mysterious and unclear, Western producers' interest in kung fu quickly decreased. It wasn't until many years later that interest was revived thanks to Chuck Norris and Jean-Claude Van Damme movies, which are actually karate stories that have technical and set developments that are very different from Hong Kong movies.

But new talents have arisen in the former British colony. We must mention film director and choreographer Yuen Woo Ping, a true master of Chinese martial arts who, despite the dramatic and cinematographic quality of his production that leaves much to be desired, is in the spotlight for creating the action choreographies of the movie *Matrix* with Keanu Reeves and Laurence Fishburne.

Another great director and expert in martial arts is Liu Chia Liang, choreographer of the action scenes for Shaw Brothers, the powerful film production company of Hong Kong.

We shouldn't forget that in Hong Kong there is also a blooming gold mine of martial arts movies with female protagonists. Of course, the supremacy is held by two Eastern actresses: Chinese Malaysian actress Michelle Yeoh (whom we have seen alongside James Bond in *Tomorrow Never Dies*) and Japanese actress Yukari Oshima.

Naturally, we cannot neglect to mention *Crouching Tiger, Hidden Dragon*, directed by Ang Lee and based on Wang Dulu's novel. With this movie, one of the dreams of the famous director came true: making a film with the typical elements of the martial arts genre but adding the dramatic quality that it has always lacked.

Philosophical Foundations

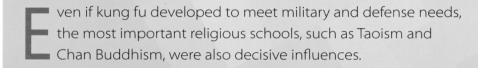

E ven if kung fu developed to meet military and defense needs, the most important religious schools, such as Taoism and Chan Buddhism, were also decisive influences.

Taoism

Since the dawn of Chinese civilization, students of Taoism enjoyed getting away to live in solitude in the mountains far from worldly affairs. There, alone and in full contact with nature, they learned to observe the universe and its laws and to live in harmony with it.

They named these laws "*Dao*," which means the path that lies underneath nature and the universe. That's why they were called "Daoren" or Taoists, which means "men who follow the Dao."

Wudang

The mountainous area of Wudang is situated in the province of Hubei, in the central part of China; its natural characteristics make it a beautiful location but also very hard to access. That's why Wudang is one of the favorite places for Taoists, who throughout centuries have built many monasteries and retreats. Wise men and immortal Taoists lived in Wudang, and many of the kung fu styles were born in this area.

Yin and Yang

The yin and yang principle is the base of the Dao.

Everything that exists in nature is the result of two opposite and complementary forces, the yin and the yang, which alternate and transform each other in order to guarantee progression.

Yin, the feminine pole, is characterized by vulnerability, darkness, and coldness. It is situated at the bottom. Yang, the masculine pole, is characterized by strength, light, and warmth. It is situated at the top.

In nature, everything is an expression of the harmonic alternation of the yin and the yang: for instance, the day follows the night as the night follows the day.

But also at noon, which purely represents the yang, we can find the yin—that is, the shade; likewise, the emptiness of the night is interrupted by the dazzling light of the moon and the stars.

Yin and yang coexist, merge, and cannot exist without the other.

Mutation

Taoists understand that everything in nature and life is mutable, such as the changing seasons, the water that flows through a torrent, or the clouds that change until they turn into rain. Mutation, understood as an incessant change, is the nature of things itself, which moves forward following a cyclical process. The seed transforms into a plant, which flowers and yields fruits that contain seeds that will turn into plants, while the fallen leaves will serve as compost for other plants, and so on. The physics principle that states "nothing is created or destroyed, only transformed" was already clear for the wise Taoists a few thousand years ago.

Taoist thinking and its attentive observations have deeply influenced Chinese culture: art, medicine, architecture, engineering, and even cooking are the result of this vision, as well as martial arts, especially the internal styles.

Daodejing

"The softest thing in the universe overcomes the hardest thing in the universe. Under heaven nothing is softer and more yielding than water; yet for attacking the solid and strong, nothing is better. Being without substance, it can enter where there is no room." (Laozi)

Internal Styles

Ge Hong, a doctor and Taoist philosopher during the Jin dynasty, introduced the concept of *neigong*, or inner practice, in kung fu.

He emphasized the importance of internal energy (*qi*), the essence (*jing*), the mind (*xin*), and the spirit (*shen*), all of which must be cultivated in order to improve vitality during a fight.

His concept laid the foundations for what was the actual division of kung fu into external and internal styles.

The external styles value the exterior effort, the use of muscular strength and athletic qualities.

The internal styles emphasize consciousness and the internal resources, where body and mind find harmony with respiration.

The most characteristic example of the application of Taoist principles in martial arts is taiji quan, which uses "the weakness to overcome the strong."

It is said that the legendary Taoist Zhang Sanfeng laid the foundations for taiji through the observation of combat between a snake and a crane.

Lei Tsu

"Under the sky there is always a way that wins and another way that never does. The way that always wins is called weakness; the one that never overcomes is called strength. Both can be easily recognized, but men don't know them. From here comes the old saying: 'The strong one prefers those who cannot equal them, the adaptive one prefers those who are superior.' The one that prefers those who cannot equal them will be in danger when encountering an individual that is equal to them; the one that prefers the person that is superior to them, has no fears."

This legend, whether based on fact or fiction, tells us that nature was an endless source of knowledge for many Taoists.

It is true, however, that very frequently the Taoist hermits met ferocious animals such as tigers or bears face-to-face, and in order not to be considered prey, they learned to imitate the animals' postures. Through this practice, the hermits were able to learn the characteristics of the animals and use this knowledge in their favor when fighting.

Taoists studied the natural forces—wind, water, and fire—and applied their principles to fighting.

Bagua, one of the most important internal styles, contains techniques that are reminiscent of the violence of a typhoon or the tempestuous flow of a raging torrent, elements of great, terrifying force.

Macrocosm and Microcosm

According to Taoist principles, the individual is a universe with the same characteristics as nature; that's why the laws that regulate nature are the same ones that regulate man. Thus, both man and nature reduce down to the five main elements: earth, fire, water, metal, and wood.

These five elements are related to one another by a generative process: wood feeds fire, fire creates earth, earth bears metal, metal collects water, and water nourishes wood. Every element attracts another and enters into a relationship with them: for instance, wood is related to the spring, the color green, the muscles, the liver, anger, etc. Within men, each element is associated with an organ (earth-spleen, metal-lungs, etc.) but also with a color, a taste, and an emotion.

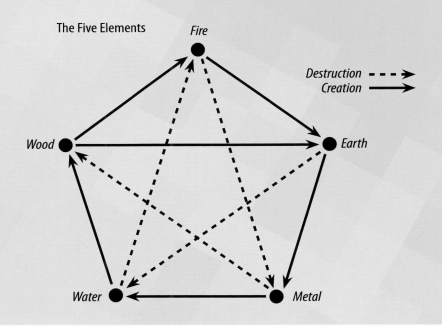

The Five Elements

Yijing (I Ching) or *The Classic of Changes*

The *Yijing* (or *I Ching*) is one of the fundamental texts of Taoist philosophy. It explores the study of the mutation principle, a concept that has played a significant role in Chinese culture. Used mainly as a divination tool, the *Yijing* offers a cosmological view of life and its phenomena. Starting from the poles, yin (feminine, negative, passive) and yang (masculine, positive, active), and assembling them into groups of three lines, you obtain eight possible combinations; that is, the bagua, the eight trigrams. Every trigram has a meaning linked to one natural element: earth, mountain, water, wind, thunder, fire, marsh, and sky. The trigrams represent the power of nature, the composition of the family, the seasons, or the organization of the state. By using these trigrams, the ancient peoples of China forecasted and obtained the answers to their questions. The eight trigrams, grouped into pairs and mixed together, form sixty-four combinations that correspond to the same number of hexagrams. According to the Taoist thinking, these represent all the possible situations that anyone looking for enlightenment regarding an existential decision might find.

Bagua zhang, one of the soft styles of kung fu, is based on the same principles of the *Yijing,* and thus, it finds inspiration in its circular and continuous moves.

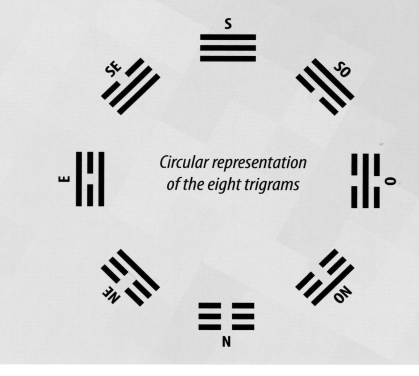

Circular representation of the eight trigrams

Xingyi quan, another well-known internal style, is based on five techniques, associated with the law of the five elements of Taoist origin, which are the pillars of traditional Chinese medicine.

Buddhism

The influence of Buddhism in martial arts can be traced to the Shaolin monastery and the vicissitudes that it has undergone.

Buddhism was founded in India by Prince Shakyamuni (or Siddharta), "The Enlightened One," and reached China in the first century BCE.

Its spread, especially among the poorest class, was a very slow process.

The Shaolin Monastery

The world's kung fu originates from Shaolin.

(CHINESE PROVERB)

In the year 527 CE, an Indian monk called Da Mo (or Bodhidarma) arrived in China, and after a long pilgrimage, he settled in the Shaolin monastery, on Mount Song, in the province of Henan. In this place, he founded a new Buddhist sect, Chan, known in Japan and the West as Zen.

The Chan sect considers that any man can be Buddha, provided that he mind is pure. Through meditation—the main practice—the individual learns to distance himself from the false thoughts that obstruct the mind, until he feels the nature of reality and the Self.

Unlike other monasteries, in which monks studied the Buddhist scriptures and were the most erudite and ascetic people, the practice of shaolin consisted of long hours in meditation and prayer. A legend tells that Da Mo himself spent nine years meditating in a cave, until his shadow was marked on the stone. There is no doubt that cross-legged meditation was long and exhausting, creating problems in the joints and weakening the bodies of the monks.

Da Mo was the creator of a group of exercises known as the Eighteen Buddha Hands, which would become the nucleus of Shaolin kung fu.

According to many historians, the practice of kung fu in Shaolin started alongside the founding of the monastery, thirty years before the arrival of Da Mo, with

Ba Tuo, an Indian monk, by order of Emperor Xiao Wen.

We don't know if Ba Tuo practiced martial arts, but it is true that two of his disciples, Seng Chou and Hui Guang, were skilled fighters both armed and unarmed.

The practice of martial arts in Shaolin is the result of other factors, religious and political, that are joined and linked together.

Since the Chan sect had a tolerant attitude toward human weaknesses, the Shaolin monastery accepted monks who were not welcomed in other monasteries because they had surrendered to alcohol, ate meat, or were warriors or criminals.

Many experts in martial arts sought refuge from society (or from their enemies) at the Shaolin monastery.

Inevitably, the practice of kung fu became common at Shaolin, whether it was to maintain a good physical shape or as a fighting method with defensive purposes.

Indeed, because of the location of the monastery—vulnerable to the attacks of bands of robbers and looters—the monks were obliged to learn to defend themselves.

Shaolinshi, the Shaolin monastery, turned into an important gymnasium for many masters, where experts could exchange techniques and knowledge with full trust since the spiritual rules of the place prevented violence or any abusive treatment.

This characteristic allowed Shaolin kung fu to improve with time and become synonymous with prestige and invincibility, but also with high ethical values.

Over the centuries, Shaolin kung fu ended up giving birth—directly and indirectly—to many schools.

The Qing era was a hard period for Shaolinshi. Many kung fu experts who had contact with the monastery were politically opposed to the Manchu government (see box on page 23); the Shaolinshi credo itself argued for the "use of kung fu to save the fatherland." Its practice was therefore used to destabilize and overthrow the political regime.

These actions led the Qing to order the imperial troops to destroy the Shaolin monastery. The monks and the residents of the monastery ran away, dispersed over China, and started to teach their knowledge of martial arts to the Chinese people. Over time, the schools diversified. Many styles were created that, despite identifying as Shaolin, had little in common with one another.

Even today the spirit of Shaolin kung fu lives on among the Chinese people, inspiring millions throughout the whole world. Every year, the Shaolin monastery attracts countless visitors and enthusiasts who come to study wushu or to revive the magic atmosphere of the place that is the cradle of kung fu.

The Manchu Dynasty of the Qing

In 1644, under the orders of the Ming dynasty, General Wu Sangui asked the Manchu, a tribe that lived in Manchuria, to help the Ming dynasty overthrow the new rebel emperor, Li Zicheng. After the death of Li Zicheng, the Manchu people took advantage of their military superiority and occupied China, founding the Qing dynasty. Despite the efforts of the Manchu emperors to approximate Chinese culture, the Qing dynasty was always regarded as usurping and illegitimate, specifically because they didn't have Chinese blood, and was fought by the Shaolin monks.

Development and Differentiation of Styles

n its development through the centuries, many different kung fu styles and schools arose and were classified in different ways.

Traditionally, kung fu can be classified in the following ways:

- According to the geographic zone where it is practiced (northern styles, southern styles)
- According to the type of force used (soft styles, hard styles, hard-soft styles)
- According to the type of mental or physical practice (external styles, internal styles)

Northern and Southern Styles

Southern hands, northern legs.

(KUNG FU PROVERB)

Each style reflects the characteristics of the place where it is practiced, the social and cultural atmosphere where it developed, and the physical characteristics of the students who study it.

In the north, where the temperature is lower and people are more robust, the use of kicks and wrestling prevails.

In the south, where the climate is warm and wet and people are shorter and lighter, wrestling doesn't have a great tradition. Instead, practitioners developed sophisticated upper body techniques. In general terms, the northern styles use longer movements and more elaborate footwork, while the southern styles use poses that are more static and arm techniques that are more powerful.

Soft and Hard Styles

Soft styles have fluid and continuous moves that don't use excessive contraction or strength, preferring to adapt to the action of the opponent rather than meeting force with force.

Drunken fist, *yaiji quan*, *liuhe bafa*, *bagua zhang*, *tongbi quan*, and *yongchun quan* (*wing chun* in Cantonese) are typical soft styles.

Hard styles possess vigorous movements and make muscles work with great effort.

In general terms, hard styles prefer to work using explosive strength and power in order to defeat the opponent.

Many of the southern styles belong to this category, such as *hung jia* (*hun gar*), *cai jia*, and *li jia*, which together constitute *cai li fo quan* or *choi li fut*.

There are also hard-soft styles, which use both hard strength and soft strength, depending on the situation. In this category we can find many northern styles such as *fanzi quan*, *pi gua quan*, *tanglang quan*, and some southern styles such as *he quan*.

The monkey style is well suited for practice outdoors.

External and Internal Styles

The exterior trains the muscles, bones, and skin; the interior trains the qi.

(OLD KUNG FU PROVERB)

External styles place value on physical practice and athletic

A Shaolin monk wearing traditional clothes.

qualities, using mainly muscle power and speed.

Internal styles emphasize the internal practice, preferring the use of tendons over the use of muscles. They require less strength.

We can also perceive this difference in the term used to indicate strength:

- In the external styles, the word *li* is used, which means "strength and power."

- In the internal styles, the word *jing* is used, which means "intelligent and refined strength."

While the li is bound to decrease with age, the jing is potentially endless and can be constantly improved with time through suitable and correct training.

The use of jing strength can be demonstrated by great internal-style masters, who are capable of defeating the most powerful and trained adversaries.

The Main Styles of Kung Fu

Northern and southern styles, internal and external, soft and hard—the number of kung fu schools is truly impressive, and it is nearly impossible to review all of them. We will limit ourselves to some of the most important styles according to their popularity and number of students.

Shaolin Quan, the Shaolin Boxing

Shaolin, father of all kung fu styles.

(CHINESE SAYING)

Shaolin is probably the place that had the greatest impact on the development of Chinese martial arts. Thanks to its geographic isolation and its tolerance, the Shaolin monastery has been one of the favorite places for men of arms: this was a place where they could find shelter as well as share experiences and knowledge.

The Shaolin spiritual faith, which did not condemn fighting but neither made it an instrument for spiritual growth, attracted the best kung fu experts who, by making vows, could retire from a violent life without giving up their own knowledge. The exchange of knowledge among experts within the monastery favored the development of kung fu until the Qing emperors felt threatened by it. As a result, many kung fu experts began to teach laypeople, making Shaolin kung fu more popular.

Shaolin kung fu has experienced constant transformations over the centuries, and the style practiced today in the monastery has little in common with the old techniques, and it is different from many Shaolin schools in China and abroad.

Soft as cotton, light as a swallow, hard as steel.

(SHAOLIN SAYING)

Technically, Shaolin kung fu (the traditional one) is characterized by simple and linear moves that can also be performed in small spaces. Hits with straight and short

Flexible and acrobatic: a kung fu student training outdoors. Chang quan *is characterized by wide moves, with many jumps and flying techniques.*

such as hitting bags of sand, introducing the fingers in ferrous sand, maintaining a headstand for hours, and hitting the body with a stick. These exercises can look exaggerated, verging on masochism, but they are very useful in creating fearless warriors. Of course, they require great dedication and great willpower in order to achieve good results.

Soft exercises require just as much commitment, and some of them are especially hard, particularly because they are based on mental control and inner respiration. They comprise exercises such as:

- *Meihua bufa*, the execution of fighting techniques by moving on top of five, eight, or nine pegs inserted into the ground

- "Kung fu for lightness," a group of exercises that aim to make the student agile and light, as though it were possible to move without gravity

- *Tongzi gong*, or "kung fu of the inexperienced," a series of psychophysical exercises that focus on training selective strength

trajectories are preferred, expressing power without showing stiffness.

There are many different forms, such as *pao quan*, *hong quan*, and *mehiua quan*.

Shaolin kung fu comprises many exercises (traditionally seventy-two), which are then divided into *gang*, or hard, and *rou*, or soft. Hard exercises usually aim to strengthen and toughen the body externally and may include activities

In Shaolin, each monk is devoted to some of these exercises, trying to achieve mastery in a specific part.

Chang Quan, Long Boxing

During the reign of the Ming dynasty, there began to be talk about chang quan.

General Qi Jiguang and Master Cheng Chongdu wrote a treatise about the differences between long-range and short-range fighting, describing thirty-two techniques to Emperor Taizu from the Song dynasty.

Chang quan has been divided into more schools, becoming one of the most highly diffused styles in northern China.

Today, the term "chang quan" is applied to ten northern kung fu schools—including shaolin, cha quan, hua quan, paochui, fanzi quan—from which it has assimilated many techniques. Currently, chang quan is considered one of the most beautiful and spectacular specialties to be found in the wushu gymnasium.

Nan Quan, Boxing from the South

Nan quan is characterized by powerful moves and basic, static positions. The arms are often stiff, while they pretend to deliver punches or hammer fists.

Southern boxing is characterized by powerful moves and static poses.

Nan quan is based on some southern styles, especially the ones from families Cai, Li, Hong, and Mo, but has origins related to Shaolin, Henan, and Fujian kung fu. Just like chang quan, nan quan is one of the biggest competition specialties under wushu forms.

Baji Quan, the Eight Extremities Boxing

Baji quan was created more than 250 years ago by an unknown wandering monk, who taught it to Wu Zhong, an expert on the use of spears who lived in the district of Cangzhou, in the Hebei region. This style is known by its simplicity and efficacy. In the past, experts in eight-extremities boxing were highly valued as bodyguards.

Tongbei Quan, Back Boxing

Tongbei quan, or *tongbi quan*, is a very popular and old style of northern China. The tradition declared Han Tong as its creator, a famous master who lived during the Song dynasty. From then on, tongbei has developed and has been divided into more schools, among which we find five elements tongbei quan, six harmonies tongbei quan, five-monkey tongbei quan, and shaolin tongbei quan.

Tong means "through," *bei* means "back," and *bi* means "arms." When delivering a hit, the force is generated in the back, and immediately after, it flows through the shoulders to the arms in order to reach the target.

The moves seem soft and fluid but are actually very powerful.

The techniques are inspired by the five elements theory and imitate some animal moves.

Baji quan *is characterized by clear and linear techniques in a short range, where hitting with the elbows is allowed as defense.*

A kung fu master performing a tanglang quan move, a style characterized by quick and agile moves, fast and swift displacements, and the alternation of soft and hard techniques, both in a short and a long range.

Tanglang Quan, Praying Mantis Boxing

According to the legend, tanglang quan was created by a swordsman called Wang Lang more than three hundred years ago.

The young Wang Lang left the province of Shandong, in the north of China, in order to find masters and experts with whom he could fight and test his abilities.

His pilgrimage took him to the Shaolin monastery, where he asked to measure himself against the warrior monks, but he was roundly defeated by a novice.

Shocked by his defeat, Wang Lang decided to retreat to the woods to meditate. While he was sitting under a tree, he noticed a praying mantis among the bushes that was fighting against a cicada. Despite its size, the praying mantis quickly defeated the cicada. Impressed by the scene he had witnessed, Wang Lang captured the praying mantis and observed its behavior when fighting.

After three months of study and experimentation, he came back to the monastery and challenged the warrior monks. Once again, they confronted him with the young novice who, confident about his superiority, attacked Wang Lang and tried to end the fight as soon as possible. But this time Wang Lang's arms were so fast that every attempt of the monk was useless. The superior asked Wang to teach him his style, which we now call praying mantis boxing.

Another historical testimony takes us further back in time to the end of the tenth century. The superior Fu Ju invited eighteen of the bravest masters to stay at the Shaolin temple for three years. He then selected one technique from each master's skill sets to include in a larger body of knowledge. These techniques were the nucleus of what would later become tanglang. Wang Lang, after studying in the monastery, added them to his own techniques, created through the observation of the praying mantis for the arm techniques and the monkey for the footwork.

Tanglang is divided into three main substyles:

- *Qixing*, or "seven stars"
- *Meihua*, or "lum flowers"
- *Liuhe*, or "six harmonies"

Taiji Quan, Boxing of Supremacy

Taiji quan is for many people the most characteristic internal style, the martial art par excellence or even the anti-martial art. It is probably the style that

A group of taiji quan students during a public demonstration outdoors.

was most influenced by the Taoist philosophy.

The earliest historical accounts state that taiji was practiced in the Wenxian region, in Henan, by the members of the Chen family. The first master of this style was Chen Wang Ting, who merged the fighting techniques he knew with the philosophical concepts and Taoist thinking regarding energy. He applied the theory and practice of the Taoist *qigong* to his style, transforming his kung fu and providing it with soft and light moves.

In the following centuries, Chen Wangting's taiji gave life to more styles.

Chen

Chen taiji is the oldest style and the starting point for all the subsequent styles. It is called Chen style because of the name of its creator, Chen Wangting.

Over the course of time, three versions of it have been developed:

- The old one, or *laojia*, created by Chen Wangting himself.
- The modern one, or *xinjia*, created five generations after by Chen Youben, who simplified the moves by eliminating the most complex techniques.
- The *zhaobao* version, created by Chen Youben, which is a later simplification of the style. Chen style consists of the study of two *taolu* (that are slightly different); *tuishou*, or "pushing hands," a group of exercises with a partner; and *zhanchang*, a group of

exercises with a partner using spears or canes.

The Chen style of taiji is characterized by slow moves that follow a spiral path, interrupted by fast and explosive moves.

Yang

The Yang style of taiji was created by Yang Lu Chan in the mid-1800s based on the Chen style. This is because he worked at Chen Chang Xing's house in his youth. He was very interested in kung fu and started to clandestinely observe the training, secret in those times, so he could practice himself later at night. But he was caught and sent to his father in order to be punished. Chen Changxing asked Yang Luchan to show him what he could do, and when he saw Yang's moves, he decided to take him in as a student. After leaving Chen's house, Yang came back to his hometown Yongnian, a district of Hebei, and became a teacher.

Since the moves were too difficult for many, he decided to simplify the style by eliminating the most complex techniques and making the moves more linear. His

Yang style is characterized by slow, wide, circular moves and by comfortable positions that make it suitable for students of all ages.

method was transmitted to his son and his grandson, Yang Cheng Fu, who further simplified the style and made it popular in China.

Wu

This style was created by Quan You at the end of the nineteenth century. He first studied alongside Yang Luchan and later with Luchan's son, Yang Ban Hou. The style became known thanks to Quan You's son, Wu Jian Quan, from whom the name was taken.

It is characterized by high positions and narrow moves, as well as by the emphasis on the arms' awareness, also called tuishou.

Wu Yu Xiang

The Wu Yu Xiang style belongs to another school. Wu Yu Xiang studied alongside Yang Luchan, and later Chen Qing Ping, the new form of the Chen style. This school is characterized by small and very slow moves.

Sun

The Sun style was created by Sun Lu Tang, who lived from the end of the nineteenth century to the beginning of the twentieth century.

Master of xingyi and bagua, he began studying Wu Yuxiang's taiji quan when he was around fifty years old, after which he created a style of his own that merged bagua's principles with xingyi's principles within taiji.

The Unifying Principles of Taiji Quan

Aside from their stylistic differences, all schools of taiji quan are characterized by soft techniques that are performed slowly, in order to allow the student to take in the movement and be able to perceive the slightest variation of state and force. The interior practice prevails

The dragon position, one of the most flexible positions of xingyi quan, performed by Master Lin Sheng.

over the exterior practice. The superficial muscles are used less than in other martial arts; taiji quan trains and makes use of the deep bodily structures.

This is what the masters mean when they encourage people to use the tendons rather than the muscles, and energy instead of strength. This forces the student to undergo a process of internalizing, which brings the mind into a relaxed state of concentration similar to meditation.

In the course of the movement, the force is generated in the center of the body and spreads through the arms and legs, where it is enlarged. Taiji never uses strength against the opponent's strength, but rather adapts to it, taking advantage of the opponent's force in order to destabilize the opponent and counterattack.

This is explained in classical texts as "using a hundred grams to move one hundred kilos."

Taiji quan is nowadays one of the most diffused kung fu styles, and it is practiced in China by many youngsters and elders, whether as a martial art or as a practice to improve wellness and longevity.

Xingyi Quan, Form-Mind Boxing

Xingyi quan is the second-most important internal style after taiji.

Tradition credits the origin of xingyi quan to General Yue Fei, who was very well known in the times of the Song dynasty. But the founder of the style was Ji Jike, who lived during the seventeenth century, known as Ji Longfeng.

His students spread it along the regions of Shanxi, Hebei, and Henan, where some differences appeared.

The styles of Shanxi and Hebei are substantially similar and comprise the five elements fists and the twelve animals boxing.

The five elements fists consists of five techniques, each associated with one of the five elements of Taoist philosophy: wood, fire, earth, metal, and water.

Every technique expresses the nature of the element that it is associated with.

The twelve animals boxing imitates the typical postures of the dragon, tiger, monkey, horse, turtle, rooster, falcon, sparrow hawk, snake, bear, eagle, and swallow.

Xingyi quan is a system with compact, simple, and practical moves, both medium and short range. It pays special attention to the study of positions, steps, and internal work with the development of the qi (the internal energy).

Bagua Zhang, the Eight Trigram Palm

Bagua (which along with taiji and xingi forms the trilogy of internal styles) is one of the most popular styles in China.

Its origins are uncertain. Some state that it was created on Mount Emei, in Sichuan, which hosts many religious Buddhist and Taoist communities. Two Taoist monks, Bi Yung and Jing Yun, might have created the nucleus of bagua at the end of the Ming dynasty. They taught this style to Tian Ruhong, who named this style *yin yang bagua zhang*.

Today, there are many bagua, including *dong haichuan*, the most practiced one.

Dong Haichuan was a teacher in Beijing and had a lot of students,

*"Subdue the tiger,"
one of the most used
positions of
intention boxing.*

among whom Yin Fu, Cheng Tinghua, and Li Cunyi were the best ones.

Bagua is inspired in the *Yijing*, the *Classic of Changes*. There are eight basic moves, each associated with one of the eight trigrams. By varying these moves, you can obtain sixty-four different techniques. Bagua is characterized by circular moves, performed around an imaginary opponent; the body moves nimbly, drawing spirals that remind one of a snake or a dragon, while the movements also resemble the flow of a torrent, fast and unpredictable.

Wang Xiangzhai, founder of intention boxing, in a picture that dates back to the beginning of the 1900s.

Yunshen, a great master of xingyi quan. After Yunshen's death, Wang began to travel around China, looking for experts to fight against. His experiences made him very judgmental toward the fighting abilities of a large part of the martial arts community and toward the method of practicing kung fu, which he thought was degenerated by useless forms, techniques, and ornaments. All of this made him create a new method, called *yi quan*. This style focuses on mental intention, which plays a fundamental role in the technique, and is based on the principles and force points of taiji, bagua, and xingyi.

Yi Quan, Intention Boxing

Created by Wang Xiangzhai at the beginning of the twentieth century, this style is also known as *dancheng quan*, or "great achievement boxing."

Wang Xiangzhai was one of the best students of Guo

Yongchun Quan, Eternal Spring Boxing

Yongchun, commonly known as wing chun, is one of the most well-known southern styles.

It bears the name of a young girl, Yan Yongchun, who learned kung fu from a nun following the tradition. According to other sources, it was her father Yan Si—a Shaolin master who fled the monastery after the

A typical bagua zhang *position, one of the most practiced styles in the People's Republic of China.*

persecution of the Qing—who introduced her to the practice of kung fu.

Yan Yongchun was training with her father when, observing a fight between a crane and a snake, she felt so impressed that she decided to combine the "white crane" style with her kung fu.

This is a style that gives priority to short-range fighting and prefers soft strength over hard strength.

Purpose and Objectives of Kung Fu

Since the very beginning, martial arts had multiple purposes in China that were not exclusively linked to life-or-death fights.

We can say that the practice of kung fu pursues four purposes:

- To cultivate character and morality
- To preserve and improve one's health as well as mental and physical abilities
- To learn how to fight
- To express oneself artistically

Cultivating Character and Morality

Kung fu is a tough practice that requires specific qualities:

- Discipline
- Will
- Courage
- Perseverance

Without these virtues, it will not be possible to progress or reach a high level. A lack of discipline makes a student a boat without its rudder, which is subject to the waves and cannot be governed.

Likewise, the student who lacks discipline will not be persevering; there will not be order in his practice, and he will be attracted to more comfortable things. This student will tend to be undisciplined in life. Willpower is like a galloping rider: one must be determined and decisive so that the horse will obey. Thus, a kung fu student must train to act with decision and determination to strengthen their character.

The student must be brave. When he has made a decision, he should not worry too much about the consequences. It often happens in fights that a good student loses because he is not brave enough and is forced to fight against two adversaries: the opponent and his own fear.

A person who practices kung fu must be as persevering as water that, drop by drop, can drill the hardest rock. Perseverance can be compared to the act of forging a sword: if you hit with the hammer intermittently, a little bit today and a little bit tomorrow, you will achieve nothing.

In kung fu, it is necessary to persevere and train without hoping for immediate results, but maintaining confidence in the future.

The practice of kung fu is directed toward physical well-being and provides notable benefits to longevity.

Preserving and Improving Health As Well As Mental and Physical Abilities

If you take care of your health you will be agile and efficient even when old, otherwise you will just be a sad burden both for yourself and for your family.

(CHINESE PROVERB)

According to Chinese pragmatic wisdom, wellness and longevity are very important for the acquisition of martial arts skills. A person in good health will be able to defend themselves even if they don't have special skills, while a skilled person, expert in fighting but with bad health, will be vulnerable.

Besides, life-or-death fights are fortunately rare today, while sicknesses and lack of health are enemies that are always lying in wait.

Kung fu experts have developed plenty of knowledge and exercises parallel to martial arts that help mitigate the negative effects of exhausting training sessions and dangerous duels. Today, this wisdom helps modern students improve their psychophysical qualities. This collection of knowledge, which is part of the cultural grounding of any kung fu student, can be divided into eight points:

1. Stretching techniques that are used to eliminate the contractures and tensions and maintain an elastic and agile body

2. Breathing techniques that increase the respiratory capacity and improve the quality of breathing

3. Relaxation and concentration techniques that help control mental activity and bodily

Exercises to temper the body are still part of the usual training of the Chinese army.

functions that very often cannot be controlled

4. Techniques to strengthen the body, including different exercises that make the body more resistant

5. Massage and self-massage techniques, which help you treat the collateral effects of the martial practice

6. Medicine; that is, the ensemble of knowledge and remedies that are, along with acupuncture, used to maintain a healthy and efficient body

7. Nutrition, considered to be the part of medicine in charge of the maintenance of a healthy body through an appropriate use of food

8. Management of energetic resources, the set of behavioral rules such as sleep and wake cycles, the distribution of food along the day, a good balance between work and rest

The common points between wushu and dance are visible in public exhibitions that are often held in China.

Learning How to Fight

Created for fighting, kung fu still represents one of the most profound and content-rich martial arts these days.

Through study and training aimed at fighting, students can learn how to defend themselves using different methods:

- Hitting with hands, feet, knees, elbows, and any part of the body

- Controlling the opponent through takedowns, joint elevations, pressures, and painful actions
- Unbalancing the opponent using fighting techniques

In addition to these methods, students can also learn to defend themselves using weapons.

The performance of Chinese specialized military forces, which apply the old principles of wushu in a modern key, impresses masters of all disciplines by its proven level of efficacy.

Expressing Yourself Artistically

Since ancient times, wushu has also been used as a training activity, whether through duels, combat, or exhibitions in which the expert performed a series of formal techniques.

The interest of the Chinese people in aesthetics helped make the moves more attractive, even introducing steps coming from dancing or the traditional acrobatic theatre, which made demonstrations more entertaining for the public.

The introduction of firearms in China in the past 150 years has made self-defense easier, but it has also made hand-combat training superfluous and difficult.

Naturally, this triggered a strong crisis among kung fu masters who, little by little, saw how their schools were emptying and their prestige was weakening.

As a consequence, in order to survive, many of them made the decision to turn their art into a sport.

Thus, in the previous century there was an evolution toward acrobatics, where kung fu doesn't seek efficiency in combat but beauty and gymnastic difficulty.

∧ Kung Fu Lesson

Now we will teach a kung fu lesson. Considering the great variety of existing kung fu schools, we have decided to illustrate the most popularly practiced techniques and the ones that are more often present in the different programs, because they are the basis of most Chinese styles.

The Greeting

Traditionally, the kung fu lesson starts and finishes with the ritual greeting. There are different ways to salute according to the style and the school. Some styles place more emphasis on the ritual behind the greeting than other styles.

Essentially, the greeting means to express a deep respect to the master, the previous masters, and the knowledge that has been passed down. The salute is both a sign of respect toward your fellow students and a sign of your willingness toward learning.

Once the lesson is over, the salute expresses gratitude to the master and to all those who have contributed to the student's progress. On the following pages, we present the four most common ways of greeting.

The Team

In the past, common clothes were used during kung fu training, as long as they were comfortable and allowed freedom of movement. That's why students could train shirtless or completely dressed, depending on the weather. With time, this need became a tradition, and in the southern styles it was common to use a shirt or light vests, while in the northern styles it was common to use long-sleeve shirts.

Today, the tradition hasn't changed much: when training, practitioners preferably use the *wushu kuzi*, long cotton pants tight at the ankles and a comfortable shirt with the name of the school; while on important occasions, such as competitions or demonstrations, they use the *wushu yifu*, the kung fu uniform, which consists of pants and long-sleeve or short-sleeve shirts made of cotton or even silk. Practitioners wear wushu or gymnastics shoes, while the traditional cotton shoes are less and less used, especially in the southern styles. Some southern schools practice kung fu barefoot, but they are a minority.

The *yaodai*, or belt, was not traditionally used in China to distinguish ranks or levels of practice, but to protect the lower belly and the lower back during training or even, as in wushu competitions, as a decoration. Nevertheless, in the West many schools use belts in different colors corresponding to each level, inspired by Japanese martial arts schools.

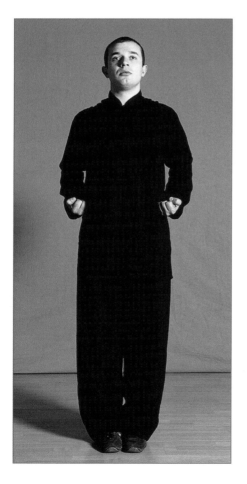

ZHUNBEI SHI (Prepared)

This is one of the typical starting positions. Feet together and fists close to the sides, with the thumbs on the outside.

Back straight, spinal column upright, coccyx slightly lowered, head erect, and the face forward. The elbows and shoulder blades must push downward.

JINGLI (Greeting)

Place your right fist in front of your chest and place the palm of the left hand over its knuckles. The body must lean slightly forward.

Many schools wrap the fist with the other hand.

LUOHAN JINGLI (Shaolin Salutation)

The schools that teach classic Shaolin from the Songshan monastery use this greeting, which consists of the hands joined together as if in prayer.

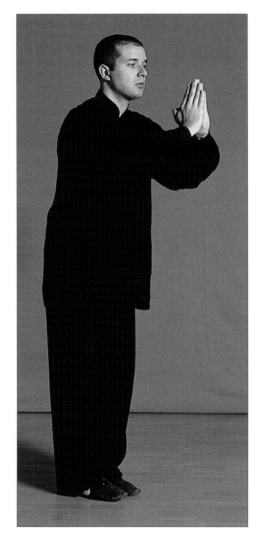

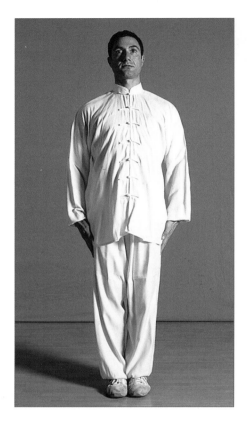

DANGXIN SHI (Paying Attention)

This is similar to *zhunbei shi* but with outstretched arms along the sides. *Danxin* means "to pay attention."

This is the same position used to initiate the preparatory exercises.

Preparatory Exercises

In kung fu, like in every martial art, physical preparation is very important.

Traditionally, in the circles where wushu is practiced, it is said: "Externally, train the skin, the flesh (the muscles), and the strength; internally, train the blood (that is, the cardiovascular system), the tendons, the qi (the energy)."

On the following pages, we present a sequence of stretching exercises that are used to stretch the tendons, tone the muscles, and improve the flexibility and balance of the body. Like *luohangong*, a well-known sequence of exercises from the Shaolin monastery, this one also has similarities with some Indian yoga exercises, which seems to point to a Shaolin or even Indian origin.

During the exercises, you must pay attention to the following instructions:

1. Remain relaxed.
2. Do not block the breathing; let it be free and deep. If the breathing tends to be blocked, it means that you are stiff or you are forcing the stretching.
3. Align and extend the spine.
4. Do not contract the shoulders.
5. Try to stretch starting from the inside.
6. Maintain each position at least twenty seconds.
7. Listen to your body, paying attention to the inner sensations.

Exercises for the Mind and Body

The Chinese people have always had a global vision of man, which has led them to create exercises and methods to improve the physical abilities without forgetting about the interior ones. Along with strength exercises, we find other exercises to improve the visual acuity and flexibility and to toughen your body, as well as breathing exercises and exercises to improve your vitality. Many of them were jealously guarded and only taught to those who were competent, prudent, and mature.

INITIAL POSITION

Standing up, with the legs together, shoulders and arms relaxed. The head points slightly upward, and the coccyx is slightly lowered.

OPEN YOUR ARMS

Lift your arms in front of your chest and open them to a horizontal position with the palms facing up. The shoulders must be relaxed.

UPWARD STRETCHING TO RECOVER THE SAN JIAO

Departing from the previous position, lift your arms upward until your hands meet overhead, cross your hands, and turn the palms up.

The *san jiao* are the thoracic, abdominal, and pelvic cavities.

The thoracic cavity comprises the lungs, heart, and pericardium, which according to traditional Chinese medicine, possesses the status of an organ. The abdominal cavity holds the spleen, liver, stomach, and the gallbladder. The pelvic cavity includes the kidneys, urinary bladder, and intestines.

The proper execution of the exercises makes the fibrous bundles that cover these organs extend, allowing a better circulation of the *qi* (energy) and the blood.

BENDING LIKE AN ARCH

From the previous position, extend and flex the trunk of your body toward the right, making the left ribs rise. Repeat the same position toward the left.

PUSH EAST AND WEST

Separate your hands and bring the arms down laterally, with the hands facing outward as if they were pushing two walls. Stretch your fingers and relax the arms and shoulder muscles.

PUSH BEHIND

Keep pushing with your palms while bringing the arms down. Lower the shoulder blades and open the chest.

BEND THE BODY TO PICK UP THE PEARLS

Bend your body forward and close your fists over the tip of your feet. The legs must remain extended and the shoulders relaxed.

THE TIGER FACING THE PREY

Bend your knees; place your fingers on both sides of your left feet and move the right foot backward. The left knee must push forward, and at the same time, the right heel must push backward, while the spine is extending. Repeat the same position using the opposite foot.

STRETCHING LIKE A TIGER

Place your hands on the floor, according to your shoulders' width, and move the feet backward according to your hips' width, adopting a pyramid shape. Push your chest toward your feet, keeping the arms extended. Push the heels toward the ground and try to keep the feet parallel.

THE CAIMAN SUBMERGING

From the previous position, flex the arms and lower your body slowly until you reach the floor with your chest. Align the body to keep it parallel to the floor, resting only your hands and feel on the ground.

THE SNAKE

Departing from the last exercise, extend the arms and arch your body, extend the chest and lower the shoulders and the shoulder blades. The heels must push backward.

PUSHING THE LEG IN THE QIXING SHI POSITION

Bend the left leg and bring 80 percent of your weight over it. Extend the right leg and lift the tip of the right foot. Push with your hands on your right thigh and at the same time, bend your body forward. Repeat the same exercise with the opposite leg.

SWINGING THE BODY TO THE LEFT AND TO THE RIGHT

Separate the legs, keeping the feet within a distance similar to two times the width of the hips, and flex your body forward. Keeping your arms crossed, swing your body to the right and to the left.

PUSHING THE LEG IN THE PUBU POSITION

Assume the *pubu* position (see page 60), place your hands on your thighs, and lower your body as much as possible. Repeat the same exercise with the opposite leg.

JUMPING OBSTACLES

Sit with the right leg extended and the left one bent backward.

Flex the right arm and place the palm of the left hand over the knuckles of the right fist. Then, push the body and the right elbow rhythmically toward the right foot. Repeat the same exercise on the other side.

Hand Positions

It is said that the quality of a martial arts student can be deduced from the position of his hands, just like the quality of a plant is revealed by its leaves and flowers. In kung fu, a lot of importance is given to the position of the hands: the hands can act as rocks or hammers, they can cut like an axe and wound as if they were the claws of a beast, but they must adopt a different form for every purpose.

Next, we will show you the most common positions.

ZHANG (Hand Palm)

Open your hand, keeping the thumb bent and the rest of the fingers straight and joined together. The palm can be used to push, to cut with the tip of the fingers, and to hit.

QUAN (Fist)

Keeping the thumb extended, bend the remaining four fingers, bringing the fingertips against the palm. Then, close the fist and bend the thumb. The fist can be used to punch with the knuckles, with the back of the hand, or as a hammer.

HUZHAO (Tiger Claw)

Keep the hand open and the fingers separated. Then, contract the fingers as shown in the picture. The base of the palm pushes forward and the wrist is bent backward.

The tiger claw is used to hit with the base of the palm, scratch, grab, wound, and push.

BAOZHAO (Leopard Claw)

This position distinguishes itself from the previous one in that the fingers are more bent and the index, middle, ring, and little fingers are pressed together. The back of the hand must be aligned with the first phalanges. The wrist can be flexed in different ways. The leopard claw is preferably used to grab or to hit with the phalanges.

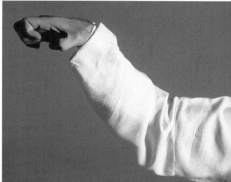

YINGZHAO (Eagle Claw)

Now the fingers are kept closed but less bent than in the other claw positions. Besides, the back of the hand is arched.

The eagle claw is traditionally used to grab, but also to scratch and wound.

GOUSHOU (Hook)

From the zhang position, flex the wrist and the fingers until you achieve the position shown in the picture. The thumb must touch the index and middle fingers.

This position is used to hook the wrist, forearm, or arm of the adversary or other parts of the body to hit with the back of the hand and the wrist, and it is seldom used to hit with the tip of the fingers.

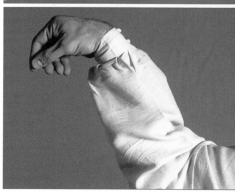

Leg Positions

The body is a fortress, and the legs are its foundations.

(KUNG FU PROVERB)

One important aspect of kung fu is the study of leg positions, which represent the foundation which every technique is built.

Every style has its positions, based on technical requirements and use. On the following pages, we present the fundamental positions, which most of the schools have in common.

During study of the positions, it is important to follow some instructions:

1. The body must remain erect in a natural way. If it leans forward, backward, or to the side, the position is not right.
2. The shoulders must remain relaxed, and the head must push slightly upward.
3. The pelvis must be balanced; it shouldn't lean excessively forward or backward.
4. The hands can remain open or closed as fists and alongside the body, or open and resting on the waist.

Use both legs and practice each position by holding it for a while.

Start by holding each position for one minute, and gradually increase the time. This way, besides strengthening your legs and back, you will improve consciousness and correct possible imperfections.

These positions were traditionally maintained for several minutes, sometimes even for more than an hour, and it was one of the preferred ways for Chinese masters to evaluate the willingness and disposition of their students.

Mabu

Mabu is also called the "mother of all positions," because it is a preparatory position for the others. In the past, masters used to make their students hold the mabu positions for multiple hours in order to analyze and strengthen character, as well as physique.

MABU (Knight Position)

Place the feet in a distance that is two times your shoulder's width, bend the knees, and lower the back. The feet must be parallel and the back straight. The position is called the "knight position," precisely because it imitates the position of a knight when riding a horse and reminds us of the sense of dynamic stability that a knight should maintain when riding. Below we can see a low and a high mabu position. Actually, every position can be performed at three levels: low, middle, and high.

GONGBU (Arch Position)

Starting from mabu, take a large step forward with your left leg, bend the knees, and extend the right leg. The left foot points slightly toward the inside (this detail changes with the variation of the styles), and the right one points 45° toward the outside. The back is straight, and the weight is distributed this way: 70 percent on the front leg and 30 percent on the rear leg.

PUBU
(Low Position)

Starting from *gongbu*, shift your weight toward the right leg by bending it and extend the left leg. The feet must be parallel, and the heels have to be completely resting on the ground.

DULIBU
(One Leg Position)

Starting from the left gongbu, shift the weight toward the left leg and bend the right leg in front of the abdomen. The right foot must point down. *Dulibu* is used to protect the lower belly or to hit with the knee.

XUBU (Empty Position)

Starting from mabu, turn your body to the right and simultaneously shift all your weight to the left leg.

Lift the right heel from the ground and bring it slightly closer to the left foot, so that the distance between the two feet is similar to the shoulders' width. The right knee is bent and facing slightly inward, in order to protect the testicles. The left leg must remain loose and weightless; thus the name empty position.

XIEBU (Crossed Position)

Starting from the previous position, shift the weight to the right leg and move the left foot forward, crossing the left leg over the right leg and turning the pelvis and the body to the left. The right heel is elevated, and the right knee is next to the inner part of the left knee. Sixty percent of the weight must sit on the left leg.

SHAOGONGBU (Low Arched Position)

From gongbu, bring the right foot a little bit closer to your body, bend the right knee, and lift the heel as shown in the picture. The tip of the foot is rotated inward, and the weight must be distributed 60 percent on the front part and the remaining 40 percent on the rear part.

Fundamental Footwork

When standing, you must be stable as Mount Tai, when moving, fast as an arrow in the sky.

(TANG LANG PROVERB)

Footwork is a key point of Chinese martial arts, and every style has developed different moves according to the technical and tactical requirements.

With the inevitable exceptions, the northern styles have preferentially developed footwork, even though the southern styles, which are more static, don't lack foot displacements.

SHANGBU (Step Forward)

From the right gongbu position (see page 59), bring the left foot closer to the right foot. Then, move the left foot forward and adopt the left gongbu position. *Shangbu* is a position used to move forward.

CHEBU (Step Back)

Chebu is the opposite of shangbu and is used to go back. From the right gongbu (see page 59), bring the right foot closer to the left foot. Then, move it backward and adopt the left gongbu position.

QIAN JIAOCHABU (Crossed Step Forward)

From the right gongbu position (see page 59), cross the left leg over the right leg, adopting the xiebu position (see page 61).

HOU JIAOCHABU (Crossed Step Back)

Once again, from the right gongbu position (see page 59), cross the left leg behind the right one. The head and the eyes must look right.

HUABU (Forward Displacement)

From the left shaogongbu (see page 61), move the right foot forward and, right after, the left foot, keeping the shaogongbu position. *Huabu* is a light and fast movement.

TIAOBU (Foot Replacement Movement)

From the right gongbu position (see page 59), move the left foot forward toward the right foot and, before the left one touches the ground, lift the right foot so that the left foot takes the place of the right foot. Then, move the right foot forward and assume the gongbu position again.

Use of the Body in Kung Fu: The Four Methods

Every martial art uses its own characteristic technical method in a fight: some styles give priority to wrestling techniques, while others preferentially use punches, kicks, and so on. In this sense, kung fu differentiates itself from other martial arts in that it uses many different ways of fighting. Traditionally, it uses four methods:

1. *Ti* includes the kicking and leg techniques in general.
2. *Da* comprises the punches and all the percussion techniques performed with the arms, elbows, and forearms.
3. *Na* concerns the techniques to grab and control the opponent.
4. *Shuai* includes the techniques to unbalance and take down the opponent.

   Among the great variety of Chinese styles, these are the ones that tend to specialize. In a natural way, some styles predominate to the detriment of others, and those are styles that fit into the four methods. This depends on many factors, mainly the social context in which the style has been developed and the election of the different masters. As we have pointed out, in the northern areas, especially the ones near the Mongolian region, the use of wrestling and control methods through elevations prevailed, contrary to the south, where the heat and humidity makes these techniques hard to practice. The personal choice of the different masters should never be undervalued: those are the styles that have inherited and adopted the physical and stylistic characteristics of the founder of the school.

Kicking and Leg Techniques

In kung fu there is a great variety of kicking and leg techniques, some of them easier than others.

Here we chose to show the most common and easiest techniques, avoiding the advanced kicks and the flying kicks which require the help of a qualified teacher.

The first four leg techniques described, *zhengti tui, waibai tui, neibai tui,* and *ceti tui,* even though they have a martial application, are nowadays used as preparatory techniques for real kicks, and are part of a group of techniques called *titui* ("throwing the leg upward"). In the execution, it is important to follow some instructions:

1. Keep the heel on the ground. You must avoid lifting the heel of the supporting foot. In general, the heel is lifted when you try to kick too high or perform a technique too fast. This can cause a loss of balance. Nevertheless, the feet must not be completely glued to the ground, especially in the kicks that require body rotation, since that could cause knee injuries. This aspect is fundamental when judging the forms, in which the movement of the feet reveals the level of the student.

2. Keep your body upright and firm. This stops the body from inclining or moving when trying to give greater strength to the move. The body also reveals the level of the student and its intentions. The movement of the body makes the kick foreseeable, which is why it is advisable to not move it.

Practice gradually, performing the techniques slowly and increasing the speed and the strength only when you have internalized the techniques.

Low kicks can be performed by staying still as much as possible in order to improve stability, strength, and resistance. Don't forget to practice the techniques and the kicks on both sides, left and right.

ZHENGTI TUI (Straight Leg Raising)

While keeping your feet together, open your arms laterally until they reach a horizontal position and push outward with your palms. Step forward with the left foot and raise the right leg, following the central axis and keeping the right foot as a hammer.

The left foot must remain still with the tip forward. Do not bend the knee during its execution and don't bend your body backward, but open the chest slightly outward. The position of the arms is used to stabilize the body.

WAIBAI TUI (Circular Outward Leg Move)

While keeping your feet together, open your arms laterally until they reach a horizontal position and push outward with your palms. Step forward with the left foot and raise the right leg, following an arch path from right to left with the right foot. Avoid swinging the body during the exercise, and keep the pelvis still.

Applications of Waibai Tui

Imagine an armed adversary with a knife tries to attack you on the right. You can use *waibai tui* to hit his forearm.

NEIBAI TUI (Circular Inward Leg Move)

While keeping your feet together, open your arms laterally until they reach a horizontal position and push with your palms outward. Step forward with the left foot and raise the right leg, following an arched path from left to right with the right foot. Avoid turning the body to the left during the exercise.

Applications of Neibai Tui

If the adversary tries to attack you using a knife, use the left *neibai tui* move in order to hit his right forearm.

CETI TUI (Lateral Leg Raising)

Keep your arms stretched with the right arm ahead, and move the right foot forward. Perform the left *qian jiaochabu* move (see page 64) and move the right leg laterally. At the same time, bend the right arm and bring it close to the body, lifting the left arm over the head.

ZHENG TANTI (Frontal Kick with the Back of the Foot)

Lift the right knee in front of the abdomen, keeping the leg bent and the thigh in a horizontal position. Then, straighten the leg horizontally and keep the feet pointed. The left leg must be bent naturally in order to achieve better balance. *Zheng tanti* is used to hit genitals, the lower belly, or the knee area.

Applications of Zheng Tanti

If the adversary delivers a right punch to your face, intercept it, grab his wrist with your right hand, and move him to the right. At the same time, hit the lower belly using zheng tanti and hit the face using *zhong chui* (see page 78).

DENGTI (Frontal Kick with The Sole)

Raise the right leg over the abdomen, with the knee bent at a 90° angle. Then, extend the leg horizontally. During the performance of this move, the foot must remain in a hammer position, and the hit must be delivered with the whole foot sole.

Applications of Dengti

Grab the right wrist of your adversary with your right hand and hit his abdomen using *dengti*.

CEDENGTI (Lateral Kick)

Start from a position where the left leg is ahead and turn the body and the pelvis to the left, adopting the xiebu position (see page 61). Raise the right leg, then extend it laterally and keep the foot in a hammer position. *Cedengti* distinguishes itself from the typical lateral kicks of other martial arts in that the pelvis and the body are not completely lateral.

That's why this technique is more suitable for middle-range fighting.

Applications of Cedengti

If the adversary attacks using a left punch to your face, intercept it, move his arms outward, and use *cedengti* to hit his ribs.

QUANTI (Circular Kick)

While standing, with the leg ahead, turn your body toward the left, adopting the xiebu position (see page 61); raise the right leg sideways while keeping your knee bent. Then, extend the right leg while keeping your foot pointed.

Applications of Quanti

If the adversary attacks using a right punch to your face, intercept his forearm with your right hand and attack using *quanti* to hit his left.

GOUTUI (Leg Hook)

Starting from a left gongbu position (see page 59), turn your body to the left, taking the xiebu position (see page 61). Then, bring the right leg forward, following a curved path with your foot. The tip of the right foot must remain elevated, as shown in the picture.

Applications of Goutui

After intercepting your adversary's left punch, grab his wrist with your left hand, push his neck with the right hand, and hook his left ankle using *goutui* to take him down.

HOUSAOTUI
(Back Take Down)

Starting from a left gongbu position (see page 59), turn your body to the right and go down until you reach the pubu position (see page 60), placing your hands on the ground. While keeping the right leg extended, make a 180° turn clockwise. The movement of the sweeping leg must follow the body's torsion naturally.

Applications of Housaotui

Housaotui is used when the adversary attacks with high kicks: in this case, housaotui allows you to dodge the attack by bending down to attack the adversary's supporting leg in order to make him fall down. Even though it is a spectacular technique, housaotui is not easy to perform in a real combat.

Punching and Arm Techniques

In kung fu, the upper body is used in many ways for various purposes.

During execution of the arm techniques, it is important to follow the following instructions in order to perform them correctly:

1. Shoulders must remain relaxed.
2. The force comes from the torsion of the body and the sides.
3. The body is not supposed to bend.

CHUI FA (PUNCHING TECHNIQUES)

Zhong Chui (Straight Punch)

With the feet parallel within a distance similar to your shoulders' width, extend the right arm forward with the fist clenched at head level, and bring the left fist to the side, turning the pelvis and the body to the left. Then, turn the pelvis and the body to the right, bring the left fist to the side, and extend the left arm forward, with the fist at head level.

TIAO CHUI (Upper Hook)

Keep the left arm in the *tui zhang* position (see page 80), while keeping the right fist on the side. Turn the body to the left and lift your right fist forward, following a curved path.

QUAN CHUI (Circular Punch)

Raise the right arm in front of the face, with the fist facing left, and the left fist along the side; the body is turned to the left. Turn the body to the right and, at the same time, lift the left fist in front of the face following a curved path and bring the right fist to the side.

PI CHUI (Crushing Fist)

Pi chui is a punch delivered with the lateral part of the fist, or with the forearm, through a diagonal move from top to bottom and from outside to inside. In the right gongbu position (see page 59), keep the right arm in tui zhang position (see page 80) and the right fist on the side. Then, turn the body to the left and adopt the left gongbu position, while bringing the right forearm against the left hand palm.

ZHANG FA (PALM TECHNIQUES)

TUI ZHANG (Pushing Palms)

As the name suggests, this technique is used to push the adversary, but also to hit them.

From a right gongbu position (see page 59), extend the left arm forward horizontally, with the palm pushing forward.

Turn the body to the right and adopt the right gongbu position while pushing the right palm forward and bring the left fist to the side.

Applications of Tui Zhang

Grab your adversary's right wrist with your left hand and bring it to the side, while hitting or pushing the chin or face with your right palm.

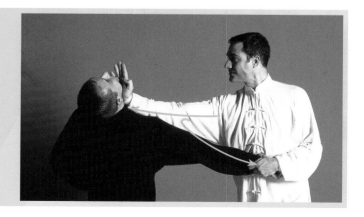

PI ZHANG (Crushing Palm)

This technique is the same as pi chui (see page 79), except for the position of the hand, which is open.

Applications of Pi Zhang

Grab your adversary's right wrist with your left hand and move him to your side. At the same time, hit his head with the exterior part of your right hand or with the forearm.

ZA ZHANG (Cutting Palm)

Za zhang distinguishes itself from *pi zhang* in the trajectory of the technique: from top to bottom and from inside to outside.

From a left gongbu position (see page 59), bring the right palm to the left shoulder and the left palm to the right shoulder. Close the left fist and bring it to the side, while the right palm moves diagonally downward and to the right.

Applications of Za Zhang

Grab and move the adversary's right wrist with your left hand while you hit the side of his neck using *za zhang*.

ZHOU FA (ELBOW TECHNIQUES)

TIAO ZHOU (Rising Elbow)

With the arms bent along the sides and the fists at waist level, lift the right elbow, which is bent, up and forward, and keep the right fist next to the right ear.

XIA ZHOU (Descending Elbow)

From *tiao zhou*, move the right elbow forward and downward.

NEIHENG ZHOU (Internal Elbow)

Bend the arms along the sides and keep the fists at waist level. Move the right elbow forward and inward, keeping your fist close to the chest and the arm in a horizontal position.

WAIHENG ZHOU (External Elbow)

Starting from *neiheng zhou*, move the right arm laterally, resting the left palm on the right fist.

HOUCI ZHOU (Rearward Elbow)

Starting from tiao zhou, bring the right elbow downward and backward, with the left palm pushing the right fist.

CI ZHOU (Elbow That Pierces)

As suggested by the name, the elbow is used to hit forward and with the tip. From the zhunbei position (see page 46), move forward with the right leg and push forward with the tip of the right elbow, placing the left hand over the right fist.

ZUDANG FA (BLOCKING TECHNIQUES)

NEIDANG (Internal Blocking)

Neidang is a forearm move toward the interior, with the palm facing upward. Bring the right forearm forward and to the left, following a curved path.

WAIDANG (External Blocking)

This is a forearm move toward the exterior, with the palm facing forward. Starting from neidang, bring the right forearm to the right, following a curved path while turning the palm forward.

Applications of Neidang and Waidang

There is a popular exercise used to practice both techniques. The adversary attacks us with the right fist straight to the face, and we defend ourselves using the right neidang blocking; afterward, the adversary attacks us with a left fist, and we block it using the right *waidang*.

SHANGDANG (High Blocking)

Shangdang is used to block high attacks to the head. Starting from neidang, raise the right forearm and turn the palm forward.

Applications of Shangdang

If the adversary attacks with a left punch to the face, lift your right arm, intercept his arm and, at the same time, bring your palm to the opponent's face.

XIADANG (Low Blocking)

This technique is useful for attacks to the body or abdomen. Starting from neidang, move the right forearm downward and outward, following a curved path.

Applications of Xiadang

If the adversary attacks with his right fist to the abdomen, move your forearm downward and forward with a curved trajectory.

WAICHANDANG (Exterior Enveloping Blocking)

The adversary attacks you with his right fist, and you block it using the right waidang move. Then, move his forearm downward and toward the interior and, lastly, push it upward, following a circular clockwise trajectory.

The enveloping blocks are techniques that are used to block the hit, but we also guide them with circular moves.

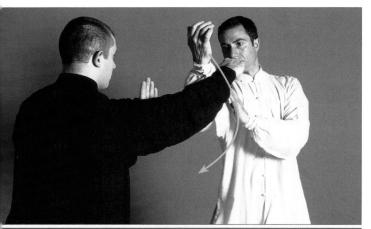

NEICHANDANG (Exterior Enveloping Blocking)

The adversary attacks you with his right fist, and you block it using the right neidang move. Then, move his forearm downward and toward the interior and, lastly, push it upward, following a circular counter-clockwise trajectory.

Combinations

T he moment has come to join the techniques that we have learned. The following combinations are only a few of the most used among the different kung fu styles, and they are perfect for getting familiar with the typical way of understanding combat. Naturally, in order to face combat, it is necessary to have learned and memorized the basic techniques explained in the previous pages.

1. GONGBU AND ZHONG CHUI

Start from the zhunbei position (see page 46). Adopt the mabu position (see page 59) by moving the left foot, bring the left arm along the side, with the right fist at head level. Twist your body to the left, adopting the left gongbu position (see page 59) and adopt the right zhong chui position (see page 78).

2. ZHONG CHUI, WAN GONG, BENG CHUI

Perform left zhong chui with right gongbu.

Turn your body to the left and adopt the mabu position while bringing the left fist to the head and hit using the right zhong chui move. The final arm position is called *wan gong* (drawing a bow).

Once again, adopt the right gongbu position, bring the left hand in front of the face, and lower the right fist.

Continue the move by lowering the left hand and lifting the right fist upward and forward with the back of the hand outward.

This technique is called *beng chui*.

Fighting Applications

If the adversary attacks with a right punch to your face, block it using the right waidang move (see page 85).

Grab your adversary's wrist and attack him while you use the left zhong chui move to hit his face.

If the adversary blocks your fist with the left shangdang move (see page 86), grab his wrist while you hit his body using the right zhong chui move.

If the adversary blocks your hit with his right hand, lower his left arm with your left hand and attack his face with the back of your right fist.

3. GONGBU, ZHENG TANTI, MABU

Move using the left gongbu move and perform the right zhong chui at head level. Shift the weight to the left leg and perform right zheng tanti (see page 72) and left zhong chui at the same time.

Rest the right foot on the floor adopting the mabu position, bring the left fist close to the left ear, and perform the right zhong chui move.

Fighting Applications

Starting from a natural position with the right side of the body forward, hold your adversary's right wrist with your right hand and bring him to your side while you use the left zhong chui to hit his face.

If the adversary blocks the punch with his forearm, grab his wrist with your left hand and move him to your side while you use a right zhong chui to attack his face and use the left zheng tanti move for his right knee.

If the adversary blocks the punch with the right forearm, hold his wrist with your right hand and bring him to his right. Then, attack him using zhong chui for his ribs, liver, or right underarm cavity.

4. FENZHOU, ZHONG CHUI, DENGTI, PI CHUI

Starting from the zhunbei position, bend and raise the right knee, adopting the dulibu position (see page 60). Bring the arms up and to the right with a curved movement.

Place the right foot on the floor and move the left foot forward, adopting the pubu position (see page 60), while you close the right fist and bring it to your side, pushing downward and forward with your left hand.

Then, shift the weight to the left leg and adopt left gongbu position, while you use your arms to perform left shangdang and right zhong chui.

Perform right dengti (see page 73) while you open your left hand and bring the right fist to your side.

Move using right mabu and perform a right pi chui (see page 79), with the palm of your left hand protected between the face and the fist.

Fighting Applications

If the adversary attacks your face with his right arm, intercept it and block his wrist with your right hand's palm, blocking his elbow with your left palm.

Grab his wrist with your right hand and move him to your side. Push his elbow toward the ground using your palm and adopt a pubu position, with the right leg ahead and the left leg behind.

If the adversary resists your control, attack his face with your left palm, so that you force him to defend himself with his left hand.

At this point, grab his left wrist, lift it up and to the right, and hit his body using a right zhong chui.

If the adversary moves back, follow him and attack his knee using right dengti.

Pull your adversary's left wrist downward and use right pi chui to hit his temple.

Qinna, Full Control

Wushu is China's unique heritage, and qinna *represents the core of* wushu.

(LI ZI MING, BAGUA ZHANG MASTER)

Q*inna* means "press and grasp," and comprises a great variety of techniques to block and control the adversary. It is an important concept in many kung fu styles.

It is obvious that we can harm an opponent through the use of kicks, throws, hits with the elbows, and strikes with the knee. However, through qinna, it is possible to control an opponent through pressure, immobilization, and elevations without necessarily causing harm.

According to its level of difficulty, qinna techniques are divided into:

- Passive techniques: These techniques are the ones used to release yourself from pressures and elevations performed by the opponent. They also refer to the techniques used against a passive adversary. They represent the most basic level.

- Active techniques: Techniques used against the adversary following a scheme applicable to a real combat. This is a more complex level of techniques that require the ability to interact with the attacker in a skilled way, fast and without agitation.

- Armed counterattacks: Advanced techniques that require the use of weaponry while fighting against an adversary.

According to the type of actions and their effect on the opponent, they can also be divided into:

- *Zhua Jin*, "grabbing the tendons": When you grab a part of your opponent's body, you not only hold that part, but you have an impact on the interior of their body, especially on the muscles and tendons, through the pressure of your fingers. This causes pain and the loss of the ability to use force.
- *Fen Jin*, "dividing the muscles and tendons": Techniques through which muscles and tendons are "torn apart" from the rest of the body in order to overextend or tear them.
- *Tuo gu*, "dislocating bones and joints": These are the most well-known techniques in kung fu and other martial arts such as ju jitsu, judo, or aikido. In general, one must apply the principles of the lever in order to immobilize the adversary or dislocate his joints.
- *Bi qi*, "blocking the breath": These are the techniques that block the respiratory

capacity by putting pressure on the neck, the muscles, or the nerves that affect the respiratory function.

- *Dian xue*, "reaching the cavity": This is the most sophisticated and dangerous phase of the qinna techniques, since it acts on the energetic circulation of the adversary.

Essentially, these are techniques that act on veins and arteries as well as on the meridians used in acupuncture. When performed correctly, they can be lethal or can cause serious harm. Because of their inherent danger, they are also called *huai shou*, that is, evil techniques.

Now we will illustrate some of these fundamental techniques.

Many qinna techniques can cause the adversary irreparable harm. The tradition states that these techniques should not be taught to beginners or to those who show an incorrect moral conduct.

KOU SHOU CHAN WAN (Holding the Hand and Wrapping the Wrist)

The adversary grabs your right wrist using his right hand.

Cover the hand of your adversary with your left hand, pushing it against your right wrist.

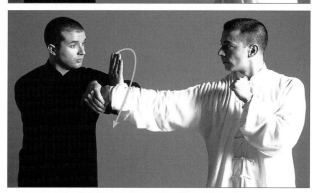

Make a 180° clockwise rotation with your right hand around the adversary's wrist in order to bend his wrist 90°.

Then, with the right hand performing the gou position, hook his forearm, push it downward, and push it behind the back of his hand. These techniques (and the following series) constitute the tuo gu group, which are very painful and effective when performed correctly.

WAI NING WAN (Exterior Wrist Twist)

The adversary holds your right wrist with his right hand and tries to move it toward himself.

Taking advantage of his force, move your hand and forearm toward the interior of his arm with a circular counterclockwise move.

Grab your opponent's hand with your left hand, resting the thumb on the back of the hand and the remaining four fingers on the center of the palm. Following a circular trajectory, bring the right forearm up and slightly toward you: release your wrist from the adversary's pressure.

Grab his right arm with your right arm: now your thumbs are on the back of his hand and the rest of the

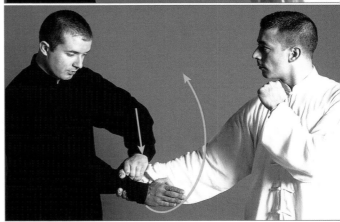

fingers are resting on the palm. Bend the wrist 90°, pushing the hand toward his face. Then, bend it outward and downward.

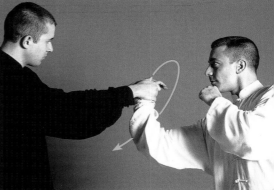

BI GANG ZHOU (Raising the Elbow with the Shoulder)

If the adversary attacks you with a right punch to the face, block it using a left shangdang (see page 86).

Grab his wrist with the left hand and, with a circular counterclockwise move, bring it downward and to the right while twisting it. Hold his forearm with your right hand.

Bring your left foot close to your adversary's foot and turn the body 180°. At the same time, raise his arm and rest his elbow in the area between the shoulder and the neck (the trapezius muscle). It is important that his hand is in a supine position, that is, with the palm facing up.

Extend his wrist downward and use the shoulder to push the elbow up and forward. The adversary will have the elbow elevated and she can be easily thrown forward.

Sensitivity Techniques

If the enemy is hard, I am soft, that is the flexible energy.
When the enemy moves, I follow, that is adherence.

(TAIJI PROVERB)

A particular characteristic of kung fu is represented by the exercises to develop sensitivity. It is often thought that these are a special feature of only a few styles, such as tuishou (pushing hands), taiji quan, or *chi sau* (literally, sticking hands). Many styles, generally the soft and internal ones, use this type of exercises.

The main purpose of the sensitivity techniques is to learn to perceive the moves of the opponent through the touch, reacting in an automatic and efficient way. In an advanced level, these exercises allow the defender to understand the opponent's intention even before he initiates the action.

Actually, the sensitivity exercises are used to train and develop the jing, that is, the intelligent and refined force, a key concept that makes kung fu a unique and superior martial art. In the Chinese martial thought, this term is opposed to the li, the force or power.

With the practice of kung fu, you develop different types of jing that, depending upon its use in combat, can be divided in three categories:

- *Don jing,* the use of energy to feel and understand the intention of the adversary
- *Gong jing,* or *ga jing*, different ways of using energy in the offensive phase of combat
- *Shou hing*, or *hua hing*, different ways of using energy in the defensive phase of combat

We present basic exercises, perfect for beginners but also very useful for advanced students.

Considering that studying sensitivity techniques is not an easy task and that only constant training with an expert can guarantee results, we encourage you to practice these exercises, always bearing in mind the following principles:

1. Stay relaxed: This is the first requirement. If we are stiff, we will not be able to feel the movements of the partner and adjust to them.

2. Do not use force: It is important that you do not use force to move or oppose your partner. The use of force impedes the development of sensitivity.

3. Maintain a stable balance: Once you are relaxed and are not using force, you discover that you are not very stable against the force of your partner. This happens because you are not interacting with the force of your partner correctly. In order to improve stability, you must act in a way that his attacks won't hit you or are absorbed by the body and drained toward the ground through your feet.

4. Adhesiveness: In order to understand the adhesiveness principle, you can think about a man in a pool. He is completely wet because of the water around him. Wherever he stays inside the pool, the water will always be over his skin. This happens because water flows continuously in all directions, toward the central axis of the person. This is very similar to kung fu, because every movement and position should move you toward the central axis of your partner.

Chanshou: Wrapping Arms

The exercises we propose here often employ a circular arm move, both clockwise and counterclockwise. Since each circle can be performed with the right or left arm over the right or left arm of the partner, we can deduce that there are eight possible combinations, four with each arm.

DAN WAI CHANSHOU TI YI FA (Exterior Wrapping Arm), First Sequence

Place yourself in front of your partner, both with the right arm ahead. Place your right forearm against your partner's right forearm, with the palm facing you. The shoulders must be relaxed.

Push with your arm forward.

Then, push downward following a curved path.

Bring your arm up, drawing a circle—in which the elbow is the center—in a clockwise direction.

You will return to the starting point, ready to repeat the move.

DAN WAI CHANSHOU TI ER FA
(Exterior Wrapping Arm), Second Sequence

Start the move with your right forearm in the interior of your partner's left forearm.

Move his forearm outward and downward with a rotating movement.

Keep pushing his forearm toward the interior.

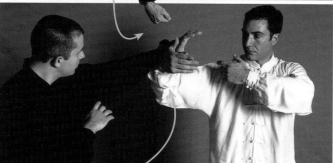

Lastly, push it upward, drawing a circle.

DAN NEI CHANSHOU TI YI FA (Interior Wrapping Arm), Third Sequence

With your right forearm on the exterior of his left forearm, move his forearm inward and downward.

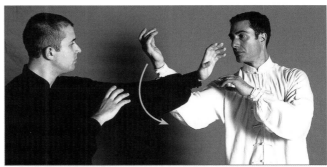

Then, push it downward and outward. In this phase, your hand must be in the interior of your adversary's forearm.

Next, while your adversary pushes with his forearm upward, place your forearm underneath his forearm...

... and keep pushing it outward to complete the circle.

SHUANG NEI CHANSHOU (Two-Handed Sequence)

This sequence is an advanced exercise: both arms push the partner's arms, with a circular move inward but a half turn apart.

Place your forearms in the exterior of your partner's forearms.

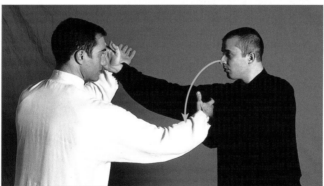

Move the left forearm of your partner inward and downward with a curved move.

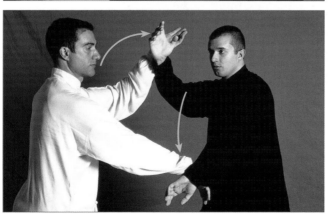

Keep moving his left forearm downward and to the right and begin to move his right forearm toward the interior. You will feel that in this moment, both forearms are pushing to the right.

While you move his right forearm inward and downward, keep moving his left arm upward with a circular move. At this point, your arms are moving in opposite directions, the right one upward and the left one downward.

Keep moving your left forearm to the exterior, while you push your partner's left forearm inward with your right forearm.

Finish the circle with your right arm, while you continue the second half of the circle with the left arm.

Sanda, the Sporting Kung Fu

Sanda is a modern combat sport that has borrowed principles from kung fu. It has removed the more dangerous aspects of kung fu from its practice in order to protect the physical integrity of fighters. It is characterized by fluid and fast moves and techniques that are performed both with strength and skill. In combat, qualities such as agility and elasticity are exalted.

Compared to other disciplines, such as kickboxing, sanda distinguishes itself especially in the different use of leg fighting techniques, which originated in the spectacular techniques of *shuai jiao* (Chinese wrestling).

Sanda competitions are held on an elevated square platform, which is reminiscent of traditional leitai, and it has precise rules: the fighters must wear protection consisting of head gear, mouthpiece, vest, cup, gloves, and shin pads.

YUBEI SHI (Guard Position)

Facing your adversary, move your left foot forward and to the left and turn the body and the tip of the big toe diagonally to the right. Use the right glove to protect your right cheek, and place the left glove between you and your adversary. The elbows and arms must protect the sides. Shift the weight to the front part of the feet and keep the knees slightly bent.

Sanda is continuously evolving, and China is making great efforts to spread it around the world. It is likely that this discipline will be included in some of the next editions of the Olympic Games.

Now we will present some of the fundamental techniques that are most used in combat.

ZUO ZHI QUAN (Straight Left Punch)

From the guard position, shift the weight of your body to the front leg and extend the left arm toward your adversary's face. The right arm must remain on guard, protecting the right side and the chin.

YOU ZHI QUAN (Straight Right Punch)

Starting from a guard position, move the right hip and shoulder toward the adversary and, at the same time, extend the right arm to hit his face with your fist. The left arm protects the right side and the head.

ZUO BAI QUAN (Left Hook)

In order to hit your adversary's head with your left fist, after delivering a right straight punch, twist your body to the right and move your left fist, making a curved move with your arm.

GOU QUAN (Right Uppercut)

The right uppercut is performed after a left punch. To perform this move, lower your body, bending your legs, and then twist your body to the left, bringing the right side and shoulder forward. Then, hit using the ascending punch with your right fist following a curved path forward and upward.

HOU BEI QUAN (Drill Punch)

Hou bei quan is a punch delivered by twisting the body. Starting from a guard position, move your left foot diagonally toward the front and to the right. Twist your body 180° to the right and hit the adversary's face with the back of your right glove.

DENGTI (Front Kick)

From a guard position, shift the weight to the right leg. Then, raise the left leg, bending the knee. Extend the left leg and hit your adversary's abdomen with the sole of your left foot.

BAITI (Roundhouse Kick)

From a guard position, move your left foot diagonally to the front and the left, keeping the tip of the foot pointing in the direction of the movement, twisting your body to the left. Raise the right leg with a diagonal move toward the left, and hit the thigh of your adversary using the shinbone or the right foot's instep.

In this sequence, we can see *xia baiti*, that is, a low circular kick. The same technique can be performed at mid-height in order to hit the sides or at a higher height in order to reach the head.

CEDENGTI (Lateral Kick)

Starting from a right guard position, raise the right leg and extend it laterally, using the sole of the foot to hit the adversary's side or abdomen. This is a technique used in sanda as an "encounter" kick to stop the opponent while he attacks using a punch or a kick.

BAO TUI YA ZHOU (Throw with Elevation of the Leg)

Stop your opponent by attacking him with a straight left punch to the head. If he attacks back with a right or left punch to the head, bend your body down toward his front leg to dodge it, resting the left forearm in the internal side of his left thigh (the glove protects the face), and grab his left ankle with the right glove.

Then, use the forearm to push his thigh downward and to the left and, at the same time, pull his ankle upward and to the left, unbalancing him and making him fall down.

BAO TUI SHOU BIE (Throw with Elevation of Two Legs)

This is a variation of the previous technique. Instead of resting the forearm in the opponent's thigh, place your left arm between his legs and rest your shoulder against his left thigh and the left wrist against his right knee.

From this position, push his thigh with your left shoulder, pull his left ankle with your right hand, as in the previous technique, and push your left hand against the right thigh of the adversary. He will fall down on his back to the left.

In order to make the pressure effective, it is necessary to twist and bend your body as shown in the picture.

BAO TUI QIAN TUI (Holding the Leg and Pushing the Body)

If the adversary attacks your side with a right roundhouse kick, move the right foot diagonally forward and to the right and turn your body to the left while you block his kick with your right forearm and hold his leg with your left arm.

While holding his leg, push his body strongly with your right arm.

Then, making use of a body rotation to the left, pull the leg toward you and push the body of the adversary forward and downward. This will make him fall on his back.

JIE TI TUI BI (Kick Block and Bending)

If the adversary attacks your body or your head with a left roundhouse kick, block it with your right forearm and, at the same time, grab his leg with your left arm.

While holding the leg tightly, use your left shoulder to push your adversary's knee. At the same time, bend and rotate your body to the right: This action will make your adversary fall down.

JIE TUI GOU TI (Kick Block, Turning and Bending)

If the adversary attacks your head with a right roundhouse kick, block it with your right forearm and grab his leg with your left arm.

Place your right glove on the base of your adversary's neck and push his head downward and to the right while holding and raising his right leg.

Place your right foot against his left shin to impede his movement and keep pushing his head down and to the right, lifting his left leg.

Your adversary will fall down on his back to the right.

SHANG TUO (Push Upward to Cut the Point of Support)

The adversary attacks you with a left axe kick.

Block it with your left forearm and place the right side of your head against his heel.

Push his leg decisively forward and upward, so that you make him fall backward.

JIA JING DA TUI (Embracing the Head and Throwing)

If the adversary attacks your head with a left punch, block it with the right glove.

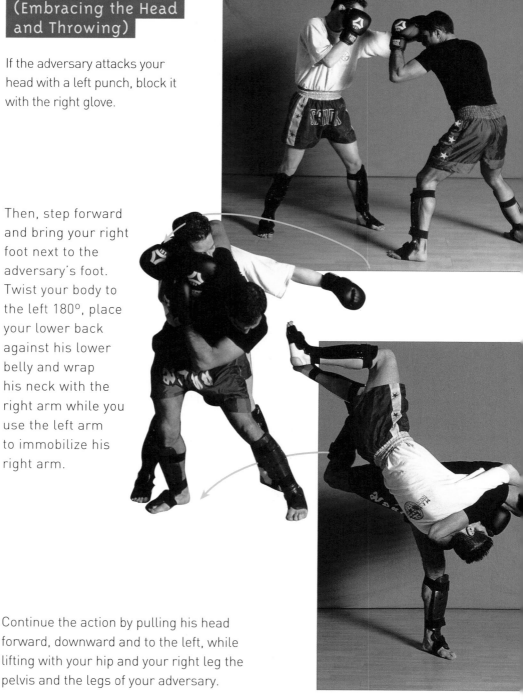

Then, step forward and bring your right foot next to the adversary's foot. Twist your body to the left 180°, place your lower back against his lower belly and wrap his neck with the right arm while you use the left arm to immobilize his right arm.

Continue the action by pulling his head forward, downward and to the left, while lifting with your hip and your right leg the pelvis and the legs of your adversary.

BAOTUI QIANDING (Grabbing the Leg and Thowing)

If the adversary attacks your head with a straight right punch, dodge it by lowering your body forward and to the left and grab his legs, resting your left shoulder in his lower belly.

Push the adversary's legs strongly toward you and push his lower belly with the shoulder. The adversary will fall on his back.

Weapons

Chinese weapons are part of the cultural heritage of kung fu. Both in the past and today, the possibility of using weapons during a combat is decisive for success. Those who didn't have a noble weapon like a sword or a saber, for social or economic reasons, learned to use objects that were at their disposal: a cane, a stick, farming tools, or even coins could become weapons in the hands of a martial arts expert.

In the previous century, be it because of the introduction of firearms or the intention to improve safety conditions, many schools gradually abandoned the study of weapons with martial purposes, continuing the practice of exercises and forms that used to include the use of weapons only by tradition.

Even though they have become obsolete in modern societies, these forms are usually a great physical and mental exercise. Kung fu weapons are divided into three categories:

- Long and short
- Stiff and flexible
- Spears

Overall, the study of weapons starts with the gun, the long staff, and the *dao*, the sword, which are the basis of the long and short weapons. Among the flexible weapons, the most well-known are the nine-section whip, the meteor hammer, and the *sanchien* or three-section staff. On the following pages, we explain two defense and counterattack techniques in sword combat.

FIRST SEQUENCE

If your adversary attacks you with a diagonal cutting hit downward and to the right, block it with your sword and hold his right hand with your left hand.

Continue controlling his sword with your left hand.

Attack his abdomen with a horizontal cutting hit from left to right.

SECOND SEQUENCE

If the adversary attacks you with a chopping hit downward and to the left, block it with your sword and, at the same time, grab the adversary's wrist with your left hand.

Prepare the hit by placing the sword behind your right shoulder and keep controlling the right arm of the adversary.

Release the wrist of the adversary and, right away, hit his arm with the sword.

Conclusion

When the wise man points at the moon, the fool looks at the finger.

(Chinese Proverb)

We hope that this book has been helpful both for the inexperienced and for the experts, if not to understand kung fu as much as possible, then at least to understand its nature, sense, and essence. No text can ever replace a good teacher, who is essential to the student when learning training techniques and methods. Nevertheless, a good book is useful for finding the answers to doubts that usually arise when practicing, and it can also encourage the student to get better.

We have tried to explain the foundations of kung fu in a basic way to allow the student to get a clear idea of the technical and philosophical content of this martial art. Our aim was also to comprehensively address the historical and cultural context regarding kung fu, so that experts and beginners can find useful information in this book and topics for reflection.

Some people practice kung fu as personal defense, others as an artistic expression, and some just to stay in shape. Every person can choose the most relevant option for him- or herself, without, however, neglecting the other aspects and the deep cultural content that characterizes kung fu. Martial arts are defined as a "never-ending trip," because as you reach your objective, other more interesting objectives will appear on the horizon.

This is the real kung fu, a philosophy of action that aims to teach students how to give their best in every situation. In the end, the technique, regardless of the school or style, becomes an instrument to improve physically and spiritually.

If we have succeeded in expressing this vision to you, if we have pointed at the moon and you haven't only looked at the finger, then we have reached our goal.

Glossary

Buddhism   A religion of eastern and central Asia growing out of the teaching of Gautama Buddha.

Dao   The laws by which the universe is governed according to Taoism.

dao   A single-edged Chinese sword.

Daoren   Those who follow the Dao or laws of Taoism.

gun   A long staff used as a weapon.

neigong   Concept of inner practice in kung fu created by Taoist philosopher Ge Hong.

qi   A life force and vital energy that is circulated through the body; plays an important role in Chinese philosophy.

sanchien   A three-section staff.

Taoism   A religion developed from Taoist philosophy and folk and Buddhist religion.

wushu   The Beijing dialect word for "martial arts," and specifically "kung fu."

wushu kuzi   A kung fu uniform consisting of long cotton pants and a comfortable shirt.

wushu yifu   A kung fu uniform consisting of pants and long-sleeve or short-sleeve shirts, made of cotton or even silk.

yaodai   A belt used as part of the kung fu uniform that traditionally was for protection, but is now more often used to indicate skill level.

Yijing   An ancient Chinese book of divination and a source of Confucian and Taoist philosophy.

yin and yang   The philosophy of everything in the world existing as a result of two opposite and complementary forces.

Further Reading

Books

Guangxi, Wang. *Chinese Kung Fu*. Cambridge, UK: Cambridge University Press, 2012.

Shifu, Yan Lei Shi. *Instant Fitness: The Shaolin Kung Fu Workout*. Chicago, IL: Yan Lei Press, 2015.

Wheeler, Ronald. *The Power of Shaolin Kung Fu: Harness the Speed and Devastating Force of Southern Shaolin Jow Ga Kung Fu*. North Clarendon, VT: Tuttle Publishing, 2012.

Websites

KungFu.Life

www.kungfu.life

A website dedicated to helping students of kung fu practice their skills at home by providing training videos and tutorials.

USA Shaolin Temple

www.usashaolintemple.org/chanbuddhism-kungfu

The official website of the USA Shaolin Temple, offering the history and philosophy of the martial art, tutorials, courses, and general information.

Index